WITHOUT LOOKING TOO FAR

MATTHEW HENNINGSEN

Bloomington, IN  Milton Keynes, UK

authorHOUSE®

AuthorHouse™
1663 Liberty Drive, Suite 200
Bloomington, IN 47403
www.authorhouse.com
Phone: 1-800-839-8640

AuthorHouse™ UK Ltd.
500 Avebury Boulevard
Central Milton Keynes, MK9 2BE
www.authorhouse.co.uk
Phone: 08001974150

First published by AuthorHouse   1/17/2007

ISBN: 978-1-4259-6230-2 (e)
ISBN: 978-1-4259-6229-6 (sc)

Library of Congress Control Number: 2006909463

Printed in the United States of America
Bloomington, Indiana

This book is printed on acid-free paper.

"Disillusioned words like bullets bark
As human gods aim for their mark
Make everything from toy guns that spark
To flesh-colored Christ's that glow in the dark
It's easy to see without looking too far
That not much
Is really sacred."

- Bob Dylan, "It's Alright, Ma (I'm Only Bleeding)"

To Vanessa,
without whose love and inspiration this
book never would have been possible

and

To my family: Mom, Dad, Amanda, and Kelsee,
I love you all very much and thank you for everything
that you do for me

Also, I would like to thank Professor Zaranka for reading
my poetry whenever I asked him to, his feedback was
always helpful and he is truly a great teacher.

CONTENTS

Introduction

All writing has a purpose: some write to entertain, some write to educate, and some write simply to remind themselves about upcoming deadlines and events. Overall, though, writing is performed with some specific reason, or purpose, in mind. As a style of writing, poetry is no different, for every poem is willed into existence through the conscious efforts of a poet. Or, in other words, every poem is written for a purpose, and for a reason.

Poetry has the unique purpose of being able to express profound thoughts in a concise manner. By concise, I mean the overall length of most poems; most poems being, on average, anywhere from one to two pages. But there are, of course, other poems that exceed two pages in length, such as *The Wasteland* of T.S. Eliot, and *The Iliad* and *Odyssey* of Homer. Also, by profound thoughts I mean the thoughts that most clearly define an idea, such as the idea of love, nature, and society. For instance, a poet may define love as being expressive of the idea of caring, whereas nature may represent the idea of beauty, and society the idea of government. Whatever the idea, a poet most clearly expresses a profound thought about an idea; in essence, this is the poet's job, and true responsibility.

It can be concluded, then, that a poem is the expression of a profound thought, and that a book of poetry expresses a number of profound thoughts. Now it must be stated that I believe that all profound thoughts, as being the integral component of all poetry, must advance change. It's easily understood that today's world is in dire need of change, but all change is futile if the human mind is ignored. An important concept to understand is that people will not change, and the world will not change, unless people change the way that they think. The mind is truly everything, and people's thoughts determine their actions. Sadly, the world has become a cesspool of perverted thoughts, and is so filled with death and dying that change has become seemingly impossible. But the poet, the true poet, has the all-important responsibility of ebbing this flood of perversion, and this flood of death, with words and ideas bespeaking profound thoughts. However, these very thoughts must tell of the death and dying that so plague the thoughts of people, for the world has decayed to such an extent that only by slapping, or rather beating, people into awareness can change ever truly occur. By this, I'm not in anyway encouraging physical violence; instead, I'm encouraging, or rather greatly encouraging, mental violence, in that the mind must be beaten free of its harmful and perverted thoughts. Through poetry this is possible, and it's the poet's job to perform the beating.

In *Without Looking too Far*, I have sought to tell a story through poems, in that each poem has a specific place and relevance as related to the overall story. Furthermore, I have broken the book up into four sections, or parts, each of which deals with a certain aspect of the story. It's up to the reader to unravel the story that I'm telling; I've always believed that an artist should never have to explain their work. True art is somehow beyond explanation. True art simply exists.

I have written to shock, and I have written to beat the thought-perversions out of heads. By doing this, I hope to perform what every true poet should perform: I hope to change this world with my words, and with my thoughts. This world of ours needs a rude awakening, I only hope that this book may be the first slap into consciousness.

Matthew Henningsen
August 2006

Part I:
A Mere Decoration

"I remember that in the beginning everything was fine, and I remember that everyone seemed to love one another. But then something happened, something awful, and nothing has been the same since."

- A disillusioned monk

Mist and Mirrors

Rising through a mist,
A finger glows warm and wet,
Gnarled with fatigue and wrinkled,
By timeless days of sorrow and sweat.

And absently striking a surface,
The finger's body creeps forward at last,
Until eyes perceive an image,
That through the mist is cast.

Yet the face quickly dissolves,
As breathing clouds the glass with steam,
And the eyes that had seen eyes,
Disappear into a frightful dream.

So alone again in the mist,
The figure and finger now wait,
Praying that the image just seen,
Will not forsake a finer fate.

Yet days of measureless time,
Become years that are not really years,
Until the boredom of waiting melts into sorrow,
And the sorrow is molded into fears.

Yes the figure and finger are full of fears,
And unseen eyes cry tears of rain,
While the finger now at last quivers,
And moves to be but eased of pain.

So viewless to all but the mist,
The finger sculpts what the eyes had seen,
And man is born then on a mirror,
Whose glass is blown a shade of green.

Yet the fingers' work is slowly enslaved,
As the mist peels from the glass,
And the mirrored man is just completed,
Before it is judged a hollow, shadowed mass.

And God can now be called God,
For its creature has been made a man,
And as such must speak by names,
That further the progress of the plan.

This mirrored man is alone though,
Yes alone as his father once was,
And to but break the silence of creation,
He paints as the Italian later does.

So with his hands serving as brushes,
And his mirrored home serving as easel,
The lone man of the world paints,
And makes Women the mother of Weasel.

And vast kingdoms are erected,
Yet scraped away before the paint can dry,
While the great memorials we humans mourn at,
Are the tombs for great men before they ever die.

And there are the wars of centuries,
That are washed away with a bit of dust,
And here he paints with sprinkles,
The words we whisper because we must.

Yet time is now time because we know,
And the mirrored man, Our painter, grows old,
And though he burns in a fireless pyre by night,
His canvases still lay There, ready to be told.

So now the father in the mist,
Is wiped clean of his mirrored son,
And alone again cannot help but dream,
And paint realities where there are none.

While unbeknownst to his slumbering eyes,
The fallen canvases awaken to man,
With a garden seen as the first painting,
Followed by a gate over a forsaken clan.

Yes man is of the substance of paint,
And lives within a canvas of predetermination,
And so years present are really years past,
And the beginning a mere decoration.

So now I sit and now I wonder,
As a brushstroke brushed years and years ago,
What museum hangs all of Our paintings?
And what theme will arise in the next show?

Escape

On a blanket of green grass,
Slender shoots still warm from the summer sun;
A tangled web of arms sleep,
A peaceful pattern spun;
And a sheet of stars,
Wraps the world up tight;
Pulsating silent music as if plucked guitars,
A string less symphony of night.

And the modest moon peeks from above,
It casting but half its glow;
While winds wash over the slumbering land,
In the forests, fields, and farms does it blow;
Yet neither the wind, moon, nor musical stars,
Can break the knot knitting two bodies into one;
For the yarn of love is as jungle jaguars:
Away from all can it reassuringly run.

Savor the Touch

"…oh babe, I hate to go…"

Savor the touch of our lips,
Meeting again after timely trips,
And savor the flush of your face,
When wrapped in loves warm embrace:
For life is far too short,
Only together can we make it long.
So hold me now as if for the last,
And gaze at me not with eyes downcast:
For in time we too shall melt away,
But in our love we can exist forever.

The Storm

They said that there is a
Storm in the distance, and that it will
Not bring rain,
        "But why no rain? I don't understand."
        Neither do we.
        "Yes, but why no rain?
        Why? What else
        Could
        Fall?"

They said that the green fields had
Rotted away, that the
Scented grasses and flowers were
Polluted for lack of discipline. They said,
        The storm has arrived.
        The storm has arrived.
        The storm has arrived.

We remember watching people being
Swallowed by blackness.
We remember weeping for the child being
Pelted by misshapen rocks. And
We often talk about the worker we saw,
Shivering as we remember the
Lobotomized stare, and the rough,
Talon-like hands.
        "But why is everything consumed?
        Why is everything swallowed and
        Never seen again? Has the storm
        No mercy?
        No compassion?"
        We don't know.
        "I don't understand."
        Neither do we.

They said that someone had
Rebelled once, had once

Fought against the storm. This
Someone, they said, had ran from the
Inviting blackness, had
Moved instead of numbing. And

Reaching a daffodil-filled cliff, this
Someone had leapt gleefully into space. So
Falling,

Falling away, this someone is said to have
Grinned (white-toothed)
Up, Up at the
Halted storm.
  "But what then? This someone, this
  Someone reclined on nothingness,
  (On air!) had
  No where to go
  But
  Down."
Yes, that we know.
  "So this someone is
  Dead? This someone must be
  Dead, having
  Died from the impact with
  Reality."
Yes...that we know.

We remember that this
Someone slept silently with leeches.
We remember that tears did not
Fall when this someone fell.
We remember that on this someone's
Grave are written these words,
  "The storm could not take this person,
  For this person chose to live free."

Yes, we remember everything.
Yes, we remember nothing.

Auri Sacra Fames

I remember the night of shadows,
Was the night the Preacher haunted our door,
And my father, I believe, was talking,
To his image cast upon the floor.

When suddenly there came that crying,
That bid us to open and to speak,
And my father and I of course obeyed,
And peeled back our door with a creak.

But oh be not deceived,
For before us hunched a benign growth,
So though it was as black as bitter coffee,
It ground neither fear nor horror between us both.

Yet it must be mentioned,
That a hand of the blackness was readily seen,
And lashed to it was a cheap, plastic watch,
That slowly dripped droplets of its spit-shine sheen.

I found it rather curious though,
That the watch told but one time,
Meaning that time past could be deemed time present,
While the future could become the present's pantomime.

But enough of this thinking,
I know that it tends to anger most,
So with an apology I shall now continue,
And relate the whisperings of this human-born ghost.

If I remember it correctly,
The figure uttered words of a broken size,
Asking only if my father knew of some secret phrase,
For to know it, it said, was to be deemed wise.

And to my utter disbelief,
My father began speaking in a grating voice,
Whispering slowly, "auri sacra fames," "auri sacra fames,"
As if, I thought, he didn't even have a choice.

It was then that the creature nodded,
And seemed to glance down at the time,
Locked on the unchanged watch for certain unchanged minutes,
Until it sounded a single, silent chime.

At hearing this my father seemed to giggle,
And wildly clapped his hands to a tempo-less beat,
While the dark keeper of time took its leave,
And skipped down the smoke rings of the street.

I then remember shutting and locking the door,
The whole time disillusioned as to what had taken place,
And turning around back towards our fire,
I felt the flames as coolness upon my face.

So with a chill falling over me,
I again found my father with his shadowed friend,
Yet now he hugged himself with confusion,
And mumbled those words I could not comprehend.

The Sacrificial Offering

Fibers rule our world,
With metal as a close ally,
Making us humans immortal,
To all but the immortal eye.

For men are as machines,
And worship on the Altar of Steel,
Yes the bits and bolts of themselves,
The ambrosia of the heavenly meal.

And cloaked are we all forever,
Smothered in clothes of our own designs,
The fiber being red as sinew,
By bleeding all that it entwines.

Yes I see humans dying,
Before they are ever born,
And those that do survive,
I see as empty and as worn.

Whole generations being blown away,
And swept back into God's dust,
And no doctors can save us now,
From the metastasis of the Rust.

So what are we humans to do?
What move will end this game?
Surely someone will come,
Who we will never know by name?

Part II:
A Pasta Shell for a
Three-legged Donkey

"It's always important to suck the life out of an egg. No one, especially me, likes anything that's not hollow and absent."

- A typical person, having been asked what's most important to them

In Search of O

I. **C**

The tree was gnarled like my
Grandpa's fingers, and I remember
That towards the end of his life he
Lost all feeling in his fingertips. He
Would rest his hands on a lit stove, and
Bake his fingerprints into cookies,
Asparagus, and sautéed
Shrimp.
I could taste his touch in a handful of
Burnt zucchini.
I picked his skin from my teeth with a
Toothpick.
I swallowed pounds of him during a dinner of
Milk and brownies.
He disappeared not long ago.

II. **R**

The apple was
Hollow.
It was
Empty like the hungry stomach of a leech.
When the
Apple
Fell,
The leech
Brushed its teeth with tomato
Paste and flossed with a cat's
Whisker. It
Squealed and squirmed towards the
Apple. It
Was disappointed though. I
Remember it cried blood.
The leech had brushed for nothing.

When the police asked for
Information about my grandpa, I
Brought them a plate of his
Macadamia nut cookies.

III. O

Jimbo, a man, is hairier than
Both of his brothers, James and Jim.
Jimbo's forearm is like
Calamari:
      Curly, and chewy, and deep-
      fried.
His chest is like a
Fresh owl pellet:
      Stringy, and bony, and somewhat
      moist.
Jimbo recently lost a dear friend, the
Black mole on his wrist. His
Hair, like kudzu,
Ate the mole with metal chopsticks and
Peanut oil.
Jimbo cries often for his friend. His
Tears taste like
Vinegar.
He named the mole Davie Livingstone.

The leech was made to apologize to
The cat. It
Wrapped the whisker in bubble wrap, and
Wrote on used toilet
Paper, "We grope together
And avoid speech."

IV. A

Jim bites the apple.
It bre-
aks like a hip.
James and Jimbo stalk and
Pounce.
Punches
Punches
Punches
Blood.
Crunches! Blood!
A yelp.
And a paper fl-
oats a-
way l-
ike a
cough.

The police complained about
The cookies.
They said there were
Scales of skin and curly
Hairs baked into them. (Had Jimbo known grandpa?)
I offered them some toothpicks.
They said,
  "No, no, no, next time bring
  Some chocolate pudding."

V. T

The paper was jagged like a
Shark
Bite.
It was yellow like a
Jaundiced chest, or like a long-time
Coffee-
Drinkers

Teeth.
On one side was writ,
    "Are quiet and meaningless
    As wind in dry grass
    Or rats' feet over broken glass
    In our dry cellar"
In one corner,
Smudged with what looked like
Ketchup, were the words,
"Hollow Men."

On the shores of Lake Tangan-
Yika, Davie Living-
Stone, the mole, has a house of
Red mud. It has been
Said that
Someone is
Searching
For
Him. But
Jimbo's arm hair dis-
solves Davie like a
Drowned alka-seltzer tablet. So Davie can't see his searcher.
Davie is blind, blind like the
Repentant leech with
Clean teeth.

VI. **O**

James, Jimbo, and Jim lurch towards the paper.
It naps, like
Christ
Entombed,
At the stubby
Base of
The tree.
The brothers
Cannot

Help but
Fight though.
They want what they have been told to want.
So each brother scratches, and
Bites, and
Plucks curly hairs from his kin.
Blood becomes their
W-
ine. And they dr-
ink into a stupor. It
Dri-
bb-
les into murky pools in the
Maternal dust,
Marking their path towards the paper.

The police found grandpa.
Chuma, a tribal man, had
Snagged him on his fishing
Reel of twine.
In the cloudy depths of Lake Tan-
Ganyika grandpas
FeetWereFused, Chuma said, into the
Soft,GeneticClay.
On one of grandpa's fingertips, a
Leech suckled
Greedily, a whisker stem-
ming from its breast pocket like a sy-
ringe. Grandpa
Bobbed
On the surface only after a
Yellow stick-e was
Pried from his hand. On it was
Scribbled,
          "Not with a bang but a whimper."

Children throw rocks at grandpa, trying to
Sink
Him.
Chunky women with brooms chase the children away though.

They scream,
>"Leave that barrel drum alone! It's
So pretty in the sun."

VII. N

Blood dri-
bbl-
ing onto the paper.
Falling like the tears
Wept for a
Legless,
Armless,
Headless infant.

So pretty!

A white arm hair of Jimbo
Laps at
The blood. The slurping
Blurs a
Word scribbled over the
Holy Uttering.

Croatoan, it reads.

Did I ever tell you that Davie
Is afraid of clowns? Or
That he eats
PeanutButter with friedRice?

So pretty! Oh, so pretty!

Or maybe that grandpa
Always ended his sentences with
I presume.

Croatoan. Crooooooatooooooan.

O. ("There you are!")

Notes:

David Livingstone, a famous missionary and explorer of Africa, was found on the eastern shore of Lake Tanganyika by Henry Morton Stanley, a journalist for the *New York Herald*. Upon finding Livingstone in 1871, Stanley uttered the now-famous quotation, "Dr. Livingstone, I presume?".

T.S. Eliot's poem, "The Hollow Men" is very important. All quotations in the poem are taken from it.

> "Are quiet and meaningless…" (Lines 7-10)
> "We grope together…" (Lines 58-59)
> "Not with a bang…" (Line 98, the last line of the poem)

In 1587, a group of English colonists settled on Roanoke Island, in what is now North Carolina. This group of colonists consisted of 91 men, 17 women, and 9 children, and was led by John White. Through a series of events that I won't bother relating, White eventually had to return to England, making it back to Roanoke three years later, in 1590. Upon his return, he found the settlement completely deserted, with no signs of violence, or even human skeletons. Everything, it seemed, had simply vanished. However, carved into one of the fort's posts was a single word, "Croatoan." White never did discover where the colonists had gone, and to this day it remains a mystery.

A Night at the Theater

I saw a play last night.
It was supposed to be a
Tragedy, but I
Laughed the entire time.
Yes I laughed so violently that I
Hacked up the cross that I had
Eaten for lunch, and began
Crying dark tears of blood.
I was the only one in the audience.

The play was
Untitled, and I couldn't read the names of the
Actors. My bloody tears,
Flo-
wing like a uri-
na-
ting elephant,
Smudged the words into a
Single,
Muddled blur.
But I do remember
Numbers in the names.
.5's and .75's I think.

Onstage, seared by
Artificial suns, cowered a man,
(A human being)
(A homo sapien)
(.)

He was wearing moth-
eaten overalls. There was also
Curly, gray body hair
Budding from every appendage.
Hair sprouting from untrimmed toes.
And hair choking his
Single,
Slender leg.

The other leg, I saw, was a
Stump. A
Stump like a midgets
Dis-mem-ber-ed
Torso, or a
GIANTS se-
vered th-
umb. The man also had a
Clear, plastic eye patch stre-
tched over one of his eyes.
And in his mouth he seemed to be
Chewing on a
Greasy remote controller.

Beside the man
(Homo sapien)
There was a donkey. It was
Three-legged and was
Shaven like a waxed kiwi.
On its sandpaper skin there was
Stuck dried globsOfClay, and,
Like the man (.), it
Wore an eye patch.
But the donkey had a
Patch over both of its eyes.
How, then, could it
See?

Did I ever tell you that the
Man
(A human being)
Had a ballAndChain
Fused onto his foot? Or that he
Beat,
Beat upon the chain with a
Plastic hammer? A
Plastic hammer with a red,
Plastic top? I can't seem to
Remember because I was already
Dri-

bbl-
ing my tears of blood, and
Because my lunchtime
Cross now slept fitfully within
My mouth.

The play ended
(.)
When the donkey
Showed his shaven buttocks.
I saw that on either cheek were
Branded the words,
Alas!(!)
Alas!(!)
Oh, and the man, the
Human being, un-
clenched his
Clenched fist to reveal a
Clear key (Clear like his eye patch).
But he gazed, horror-
stricken, at the key. His
Left eyelid twitched like a
Blown-
off leg. So he
Quickly clenched his fists again,
Smiling yellowed teeth, and
Resumed his
Beating,
Beating,
Beating on the chains.

I got up then,
Jesus saving my seat, and went to
Buy some gummy bears
For the next
Show.

Eyeglasses, Inc.: Daily Minutes for December 25

We are absent here,
Here, there is nothing...nothingness, alas!
Those who have come here
Leave empty,
Leave like a hollow pasta shell,
Like a mouse eating a needle that was
Vomited up by a blind boy, who
Had his stomach stapled.
No one could hear the needle, though,
No one could hear it at all, not at all.

I think the needle spoke Swahili, but
I can't be certain,
Here, I can never be certain.

These fries need salt,
But here there is no salt,
There is only water, bland and hot.
"Don't eat your salt, deary,
No please don't, it'll only make your
Stomach ache."
    "Okay, Ma, I won't, I promise that
    I won't."

Why won't the blind boy look at me?
I must have a zit.
I'll pop it after class with the
Mouse's needle.

My Ma has been dead for nine years.
She died of an oversized goiter,
It looked like she had two heads.

One night the goiter said "Zoom!"
And I was afraid.
I hid under my bed for days, eating

Stale popcorn and pocket lint.
Ma made the goiter finally apologize
Though, and I remember it winked
At me.

"That's a good deary, good deary,
Good deary, will you set some
Water to boil, I'm thirsty."
Thus spoke the goiter. Or was it Ma?
I can't tell anymore who is speaking.

I want to pop the goiter with a needle,
But I can't find the mouse, it has
Disappeared into its hole and only leaves
Round turds like kidney stones for me.

Franklin, the blind boy, plays
Chess every Sunday with
Abe, the mute midget.
Abe says Franklin cheats.
Says Franklin eats his pawns with
Cottage cheese and holy water.
But I can't tell.
Here, I can never tell.

Abe died of a
Heart attack when he met Ma.
His mouth bled salt water.
Who is that playing chess with Franklin then?

I think that the mouse stole my salt, and
That he is hoarding it with a roach
Called Sally.

But why does Sally call me deary?
And why does she grin at me like
A fat man with a fudge bar?

The blind boy said he saw me
Fishing last night. He
Caught a trout, I
Caught a doll, it said, "Go west, young man."

I should go and skip rocks in a
Dry river bed.
I should rename myself Adolph and
Move to Brazil.
I should whittle a cross with a
Fork in my bathtub.
I should grow a beard, and dress in
A long robe, and anoint people with
Barbecue sauce.
I should eat a peach.

Zoom! Zoom!

"Deary, will you scratch my back,
The goiter can't reach?"

Zoom!

Easter

A fishing-pole floats,
On a pond hugged by a farm,
And unreeled is its line,
And bent straight its broken arm.

A child is then skipping,
An arm hooked over a basket,
And inside there is a lonely egg,
Like a rat in a dead man's casket.

Desert hands choking the egg,
As sand on a parched throat,
While a slender needle inoculates the white,
And lips kiss the wound they smote.

So now slurped is the yolk,
And gurgled the creamy albumin,
Until spat is the mixture of life,
Into a cold sink of tarnished tin.

But the hollowed shell is placed aside,
Waiting to be wrapped in a color of dye,
Like naked bodies waving naked hands,
That sink in supplication under the sky.

An Always Playing Play

Acts I-V.
(*spoken softly, almost at a whisper*)

"Some stand and see
What is not really there,
While others look,
And glimpse only air.
Yet all are privy
To the wonders rarely seen,
Yes, vast worlds of wisdom
Where knowledge reigns supreme.

(*even softer now, now almost a sob*)
And it is sad, then,
That so many are blind,
And the changes left unchanged,
Are forever blotted from the mind.
For we all look, and we all see the same day,
Genius is merely to sit, and to watch a hidden play."

Words from a Padded Cell

"It's nice to have someone to talk to,
Even if there's no one there,
And alone speak through,
The fog that fills the air.

For often when I sit with others,
And try to show them my mind,
Each closed self smothers,
All thoughts of a foreign kind.

Yet blame is not to be dealt to one,
For all bear the brand of guilt,
Each a victim of the garrison,
That wages war for a society in selfishness built.

So I am as a rebel,
An enemy fighting from the mind,
Unwilling to slumber with each pebble,
That chokes the marshes of mankind.

And though each day brings a darker night,
And victims numberless still pile higher,
I cannot falter from the fight,
For few remain to douse the fire."

Meeting Marty

The man with the bloody teeth approached me.
His nametag read,
    "Hello! My Name Is
        Marty
      What's Yours?"
It too was bleeding,
As if it were pinned into
Marty's pale, flaky skin.

Marty tried to speak, but he
Couldn't.
Couldn't.
His severed tongue, like a
Hooked tuna seen convulsing on shore,
Only flapped, up-and-down,
Up-
and-
Down,
Up-and-
Down.
It looked like it was waving, I thought,
And so I waved back, my
Fingernails untrimmed.

Marty made only two movements. He
Pointed at himself, and he
Pointed at the other people walking by.
Just
Walking by, his finger seemed to say, as it
Twitched with spasms like the
Tuna. Looking, my tongue
Limp and dry, I saw Marty's yellow shirt. It was

Speckled, like a sprinkled cookie, with
Drops of
Freshly-oozed blood. Marty's other
Finger was pointing at the walking people.
They were
All
Clad, I saw, in
Tight-fitting, white shirts, noticeably
Starched and
Pressed.

"White.
White.
White!" Marty mumbled, as he
Choked on the fragmented
Bits of his pink tongue.

He stumbled away then. I remember he was
Crying. I remember he was
Searching for something in his back pockets.

What was Marty searching for, I wonder?
What could it have been?

What? What?

What?

Part III:
Land of the Free,
Home of the Brave

"I've always believed that the United States of America is God's gift to mankind, and that no where in the world is there a country more educated and free."

- A famous patriot, delivered upon the outbreak of another war

Lumpy Milk

Riding a bike.
The road rough and abrasive like
An unshaven chin.
In the distance there is a cow – it's
Speckled with white and black
Splotches; it looks like an
Oreo with teats, I think.
This cow is giving birth. I hear the
Screeching moo's, and see the
First faint forms of the calf's
Sticky head.

I wonder as I roll by: Could this be the
Promised One? The One that
Teachers teach to us, and that
Preachers preach to us?
      "Wait! Wait! Wait!" they cry,
      "Wait!"
      "Soon it will come!"

They have been saying that for
Centuries now, and
Still I wait.
Still I pedal on,
Looking,
Searching,
For a cow?

Taking Tea with Aunt Jane

Drifting on chilled mountain water,
I contemplate a moss-pebbled lake floor,
And so hear the adrenaline clamor of a key,
Turned menacingly in an already unlocked door.

And swinging open that which has long since been ajar,
I view but the same algal stones,
That have been weathered many a minute,
By the bleached bits of crushed cranial bones.

And Aunt Jane said, as she plucked
      my cheap fiddle,
"The dead shall rise again! The dead shall rise again!
      So early in the morning,
      So early in the morning,
      So early in the morning,
      Before the break of day."

Now as the water is clear and cool,
And the sun above shines so bright,
My Michelangelo gaze* into the depths,
Is hazily reflected before my sight.

So as I study bone-beaten rocks,
And childishly massage their still-slick slime,
My own misty image is seen scratched,
Into the slow-creeping mosses of time.

But before I can learn from myself,
A motored boat slices through the water,
As does a dull knife sink into soft butter,
And a well-ground neck blade shorten the line of slaughter.

Yes I am now, I fear, forever muddled,
And I can no longer see my mossy me,
And so I must learn to forget the face that
Had promised to teach me all I could be.

And as the sun fell, Aunt Jane said,
      as she handed me another cup of tea,
"Let the dead bury the dead! Let the dead bury the dead!
      So early in the morning,
      So early in the morning,
      So early in the morning,
      Before the break of day."

* see Raphael's *School of Athens,* the figure sitting in the lower
center, his elbow resting on a marble tablet, a quill in the
other hand.

Modern Warfare

Modern warfare is fought not
On a distant hill,
Nor in an equally distant country,
With the young dying for others,
Others who they never met,
And never will.

For bullets are shot at
The citizens of a country
From guns held by the hands
Of a fellow countrymen,
From the hands of a wife, a son,
A neighbor, and a friend.

Death is so common these days
We no longer feel numbness, nor pain
At the dead and the dying,
At bodies without heads,
Or heads without eyes,
Or heads without brains.

And to see such death,
To drown in blood and in tears,
All we need do is look to our
Fellow countrymen as the suppliers,
The executioners, the damned,
The doomed, the lost.

So when you see a gun,
Or a cartridge lying empty,
Know that it is wartime,
Not in some distant country,
Instead look around you and tremble,
For the enemy is already at your doorstep,
    Gun cocked and loaded.
Knock.
Knock.

Band Camp

"...those not marching to their
tune they call it treason..."

We were all marching again,
Marching
(All of us) on that
Dirt field. We looked like
People with a purpose, like
People marching,
Marching towards some
Great goal, towards some
Great end. But
We were really only following the
Directions of the conductor.
Marching in step, yes
Always
Marching in step
Despite his sudden
Spasms of fury and
Those times when
Page after
Page of
Music were conducted
With a wrinkling of the
Forehead, and a
Squinting of the eye.
       "Stay in step.
       Stay in step. Oh,
       Always stay
       In
       Step," he screams.
So we
Stay in step.
Always.

You never liked him much, the
Conductor.
You always said that he smelled
Like moth-
eaten mothballs.
You always said that he
Acted like a pen:
        Narrow-tipped, and
        Preloaded with a permanent
        Stain.
But more than anything, you
Despised his selection of music, saying,
        "Why, why is it the same song
        Repeated over, and
        Over, and
        Over? Doesn't anyone else
        Notice? Doesn't anyone else
        Care?"
We didn't know,
We knew
Only to keep in step. Yes
Always to keep in step.
Always.

We remember when you were
Tripped, fall-
ing to the ground. You had tried to
Break free of our fixed form,
Had tried to
March to a
Beat unknown to
The conductor.
And so
You
Fell,
Denting your horn and
Skidding your knee.

(We remember the blood, the
Dark droplets dri-
bbl-
ing off your shoes,
Pit-pattering,
Pit-pattering onto the ground)
But everyone else kept marching,
Beating,
Beating,
Beating their feet in time.
Yes always in time, their feet.
Their feet always in time.
Always.
Always.
Always.

You told me once that you had
Heard two things while on the
Ground. First, yes first, you
Told me about the music, saying,
        "One line
        Drif-
        ted by,
        One line
        From the song that
        Everyone
        Always played.
        I remember the lyrics:
        …O'er the land of the
        Free and the
        Home of the brave…
        Yes I remember these were the
        Lyrics I heard when I laid
        Tripped and
        Sprawling on the ground."
You also said that a
Chunky tuba player, dressed in

Faded reds, and
Whites, and
Blues, had
Hacked three words at you,
He had said,
    "Traitor,
    Traitor,
    Traitor!"

And all of this while you
Were on the ground, yes
On the ground with a
Dented horn and a
Bloodied knee.

An Interview with a Soldier of God

"everyone says God is on his side…"

Tell me what the problem is.
Tell me why you are
Eating your fingernails as if they were
A delicate dish of
Week-old ham and st-
ring ch-
eese.
What could have happened to
You yesterday?

Shot a man, shot! shot.
Shot
Shot
Shot a man. Shot!
Blood, blood was everywhere
Shot!
Blood in my hair,
Shot!
Blood on my shirt,
Shot!
Blood in my mouth,
Shot! Shot!

Who did you shoot? I
Hope it was one of
Those people,
Those that we are told to
Shoot.

Shot me a brown
Man of the desert. Brown
Man dressed in black.
Brown man.

Man,
Just like me.
Shot!

Was this
Thing dead? Or was this
Thing only wounded?

Brown man only shot. Brown
Man only shot near the
Heart. Brown man
Hacking up blood, and
Mumbling, only mumbling

What? What was the
Thing mumbling?

In perfect English, brown
Man mumbling,
      "I thought God was on my side,
      I thought God was on my side,
      I thought God was on my side,
      I...God...my side, side."

Allah be praised! I can't
Believe it, no I can't
Believe it at all! That
Thing said that? Great
God!
But what then did you do?

Shot me dead that brown
Man.
Bang!
Shot him
Good-and
Dead.

Shot brown
Man right in the head,
Three times.
Bang!
Bang!
Bang!
Brains everywhere.
Brains in my teeth. Brains
Mixing with the blood, forming a
Lumpy soup.
I forgot my spoon though.

Delicious! Delicious!
But why did you shoot
Him again? The
Thing would have
Died on its own.

Shot him dead because
God,
God's on my side, and
I wanted him to know that.

Of course! Of course!
Very well done, yes
Very well done indeed!
But don't you
Forget that.

Oh, don't worry!
I won't.
I won't.

Obituary for July 4

You walked the streets today.
You walked
Them and saw the
People,
Those people wearing clothes looking like
Steamrolled piles of
Brown and
Green dog dung. Don't
You remember?
They nearly
Marched over you, trying to
Stomp out your brains with their
Steel-toed boots.
You remember,
Right?

You whispered,
Hiding your lips with your hands,
        "Why do they wear such
        Thick glasses? It makes their eyes
        Bulge like the blOATed bODies
        Of the overnight dead. And all-
        seeing like that
        Eye on the back of the
        Dollar bill. You know
        That eye at the top of
        That pyramid?"
We didn't know,
We never know...
        At least not anymore.

You kept on walking, staring
Down
At the paper-patched streets.
Your eyes read the foot-

printed paper. Read through the
Smudged words and
Blacked-out numbers.
(Were they numbers of death? Death counts?)
(We weren't sure,
        No, we weren't sure at all)
You read aloud, describing the
Wars waged for
Some God, and about the
Men and about the
Women and about the
Children that were all
Butchered and baked and
Skinned and impaled for
Some God.
        "Some God," you mumbled again.
Some God.
You then asked whether this
God was really
One God, universal to all.
We said we weren't sure,
That we had been
Taught to believe
In a variety of Gods, and in a
Variety of peoples.

You looked up at
Those people.
Bli-nking.
Bli-nking.
You skipped over to us, and
Whispered into our ears
(Your voice warm against our ears)
        "Why, why do they
        Baste themselves with sunscreen? Can't
        They see that the day is as dark as a
        Lodged bullet? A lodged bullet

Lodged within the brain? Shouldn't their
Glasses allow them to see
Better? To see farther?"
We shook our heads,
Dumbfounded.
Saying that
We didn't know,
We never know...
    At least not anymore.

You then pointed
(Your fingernails painted yellow)
Up,
Up at the black clouds of the
Approaching storm.
You shouted, for
All to hear,
    "Look! Look at
    Those clouds! Don't they look
    Exactly like
    Those people?
    Exactly. See how they
    March,
    March ahead, wearing
    Thick, steel-toed boots. And
    How their clothes too are
    Slick globs of flattened
    Dog dung. See look!
    Look! Why aren't
    Those people looking?
    Shouldn't they at least
    Worry about the rain?
    Shouldn't they at least
    Get themselves some
    Umbrellas?"
We sighed heavily, wiping a
Thick tear away.

Saying that
We didn't know,
We never know...
      At least not anymore, but
      Told you not to worry about the
      Umbrellas, because it
      Wouldn't be
      Rain that
      Would
      Fall.

A Letter from Dear Uncle Samuel

"How long is a day in the dark?
Or a night drowned forever in sunshine?"

These questions I ask as I sit in a park,
Watching an army of black ants charge in a narrow line.

The fat ants stumble along quickly,
Moving as if they had some great enemy to fight,
While the few that fall behind, wearied and sickly,
Are gorged open by spiny feet of ferocious might.
Then looking ahead as to what the ants were marching to,
I saw a gaping hole, dark and deep,
Yet the ants showed no signs of stopping- I wondered if they knew
That ahead there was a chasm from which they could not creep?

Then I looked up and saw humans milling mindlessly about,
Trampling ahead like the ants, without a fear, or a doubt.

Yours truly, and with the warmest of regards,
Uncle Sam

Part IV:
Drink your Oil,
Drink your Oil,
Drink it Good and Fast

1. Empty all vital fluids into a metal pan.
2. Replace with at least 6 pints of low-grade oil.
3. Repeat as needed.

- A best-selling self-maintenance guide

Pas de Escargots Pour Moi, Merci

What if our minds are arenas without chairs?
Only hollow, pink balls
Studded with dark holes,
Studded with dark holes that
Disappear into
A lonely distance?

And on a membrane balcony
A reader recites words,
Speaking to the hollow ball,
Words, songs, and phrases bouncing
Off of the pitted walls, and
Disappearing into the
Cold darkness.

And in this ball of
Nothingness,
The reader taps a
Microphone,
          Tap! Tap!
          Thud.
          Thud.
A hollowness of sound
(Thud.)
Much like the
Hollowness
Of space within the pink ball.

And if this is the case,
If a reader is on a
Membrane balcony, and
If a reader is
Speaking to a hollow,
Pink ball,
(A pink ball of nothingness)
Then words, songs, and phrases become
As dark and as cold as
The pitted walls which
Swallow them,
Slurping them
As one
Slurps runny escargots
(Runny escargots with butter on the side.)

So to ensnare
Words, songs, and phrases,
The dark holes must be
Welded shut.
Oh, and be sure to return the
Escargots, and ask instead for a
Plump filet
(Cooked medium well, of course).
　　　"Bien Sur!"

What Sid, the Ascetic, Said

"We drive a path,
And it is paved,
It is defined and marked,
It is well traveled too.
And no one looks
Out of the glass,
No one sees into
The distance,
Looking not, I say, at
The fields, and at the colors.
No one can see this,
And it is a pity,
For the distance is calm,
And quiet, and filled with breeze and rustles.
So this is where I want to be,
(Yes, I'll leave right now)
I don't want to be in the front,
In the lead of an army,
I want nothing of it,
I want nothing of it at all.
I want only the distance,

And the hills, and a
Solid walking stick.
Yes, I want to crash on the path,
I want to be thrown from it,
Belched from it,
Heaved from it,
And land bruised and bloodied,
And full of pain,
And only then, I think, can I be
Truly free,
For pain must follow freedom into the distance
(Write that down for me,
Here on this piece of paper)
It is the only way to break free,
The only way to live by dying,
Yes, the only way to truly live.
Oh, can I have that piece of paper now?
It'll certainly come in handy."

The Purifying Ritual, or Words from a Noble Savage

It is now time to depart,
I say be cleansed of the cancer,
Yes go into the boundless wilds,
And there, there seek the answer.

For this world is but a shadow,
An image forged by greed and by pain,
And we humans in it act as gods,
And squat here during our righteous reign.

Yes we humans glimpse the eyes of space,
And delve into the cells of cells,
Yet we are blind to our own kind,
And speak but at parting knells.

So flee from the captor of ages,
The pollutant of all things sublime,
And fade freely into the welcoming woods,
Where all exists except time.

And here there will be a cleanliness,
A purification of that most muddled slate,
And the Mother of old shall serve as guide,
As we search for that Highly guarded gate.

Yes the savage shall be ennobled,
And converse with the moon and the stars,
While the machine is at last disassembled,
That most had confused with bars.

So why waste time dying?
Why drink from the half empty glass?
Are we humans to be but actors
In the staging of death's death Mass?

I for one hope not,
And pray that the past shall rise again,
Yes time old will become time new,
And the savage shall love the pen.

A Eulogy for W.A. Human, Drowned in a Tub of Oil

"The Horror! The Horror!"
-Tribesman Kurtz

Number .016 you are slowing down.
Tell me why Number .016?
> Are you rusting?
> Do you need more oil?
> Or maybe it's a screw come loose?
Oh, what is it Number .016? What is it?
Don't you know that time is money? You should!
Shouldn't you?

Here come the pieces Number .016.
Reach for them now and stuff them.
Don't you know that's your job .016?
Don't you remember these pieces here in my hand?
See look here, look at them.
> Yes, come here, it's alright.
See, ah-ha, here, here's a metal screw!
And there's a tiny tightening bolt!
See look at them! Look!
Don't you remember?
Oh, how could you forget *them* Number .016?
How, I ask?
How?

Never mind that Number .016,
Never mind that at all.
I'm absolutely certain that you can be cured,
Yes I myself will reprogram you.
So come here Number .016,
Come to me and I'll make everything alright.
> Oh, I promise, I swear to you that I will!
For have I ever lied to you Number .016? Have I?
If anything you should be grateful to me.

Yes, you should worship me here
In this factory of well-oiled parts.
So I demand,
No I command you Number .016,
As if on polished steel tablets to come here!
Come to me as your creator and destroyer,
Yes, your ultimate doom!
But come, everyone else has, Number .016.

The oil is ready to be poured as blood,
And the wrench feverishly trembles in my hand.

This won't hurt at all, Number .016,
No, this won't hurt a bit, I swear!
Just a quick loosening here,
Then a little turning there,
And, Voila! My masterpiece unveiled!
But it is here, Number .016,
Yes, here in your machinery of the mind,
That there lurks a most grievous abnormality, a mutation,
Like breathing slime squirming from dry dust.
Oh, it is truly hideous, truly disgusting!
But above everything Number .016,
Your so-called mechanical evolution
Is far too civilized, far too human-like,
And that, Number .016, is unacceptable,
Yes that is forbidden, condemned,…treason.
But again I tell you to fear not,
For I shall rescue you from the thinking
That is like a featherless bird slowly
        pecking at espoused, sun-burnt intestines.
And, what's more, the change is so simple
Number .016.
Yes all I need to do is snip a few chains,
And quietly disassemble a few unneeded wheels.
Of course, though, there will be the blood that
        oozes from the amputated metal chains.

Oh, I despise blood Number .016!
For it makes me jealous, and upsets the bolts of my stomach,
As if nails and screws were slowly pureed in a cheap, plastic blender.
But enough of this mechanical blathering.
Yes, it has come to pass that you, Number .016,
(As He points with an extended index finger)
Are now to be rendered Holy amidst your fellow metal disciples.
So bow down to me, Number .016,
And softly kiss my well-oiled, unfeeling toes!
Then I will begin my rude surgical removal of your viral humanness.

...And now the first snip Number .016,
Oh, My! What a spurt of blood!
Yes, what a jet of blood indeed!...

You are most certainly better Number .016.
I have never seen you stuff so fast!
        How nimble and calculating are your fingers,
        How thoughtless are your eyes!
It is truly a miracle .016,
Yes it is marvelous, righteous, accepted!
Oh, that reminds me,
It would be tragic to forget,
I have brought you a new canister of oil.
        Now be careful with it.
I wouldn't want to anoint you again,
        Now would I Number .016?
Anyway, just remember what I told you
If you are ever to question, or think, or feel:
        "Drink your oil, Drink your oil,
        Drink it good and fast,
        Yes, Drink your oil, Drink your oil,
        Drink it to the last."
Well Number .016 it's been a pleasure conforming you,

But now I must depart and help others like you.
        No one likes a whole number, you know!
Oh, one more thing though,
Probably the most important thing,
I'll be sure to bill you for my services of salvation,
And, of course, for the oil Number .016.
Yes, I can't forget the oil. Oh God no!
It is so important, so necessary, so…
        purifying.

Well goodbye Number .016!
        Yes, bye, bye, goodbye,
            bye, goodbye, bye…
                bye…good-…
Tah-tah!
(He is swallowed by the steam from the machines,
And gradually only distant whistling is heard.)

www.ingramcontent.com/pod-product-compliance
Lightning Source LLC
Chambersburg PA
CBHW021244280526
45784CB00005B/2233